GW00655896

©2018

'Creating a Shape for Life to Flow'
Published by: Stephen Hill - Ancient Future 2018

Cover design & layout by Tom Carroll

ISBN: 978-0-473-46541-4

Creating a Shape for Life to Flow is available from
www.amazon.com

More resources can be found at:
www.ancientfuture.co.nz

ANCIENT
FUTURE

Creating A Shape For Life To Flow

BY STEPHEN HILL

I have decided to write this little book to help our transition into a new life in the Father's love. What throws many people off track is that sonship looks a lot different to servanthood. In servanthood, there was a lot of activity to be involved with, and little need to seek our own direct revelation from the source, but sonship is different. You have to learn to breathe the rarified air of freedom.

When we lived out of a predominantly servant-hearted motivation, there were plenty of institutions, organisations and programmes of activities to fit into. Or we may have had many things to do because we felt that we should do them, or in obedient response to a command from the Lord. However, when we come into the ongoing experience of being loved by the Father, many of these activities drop off, because our hearts are no longer motivated to engage in them. This new reality brings its own challenges, and I have noticed within myself and in many others, a tendency for discouragement and confusion. The big question is: "What happens now?"

The first thing to do, is to do nothing. Simply learn to receive and keep on receiving the Father's love. The default stance of sonship is to be positioned downstream from its Source, the Father. Sons and daughters never, ever stop receiving. All that is from heaven and from the heart of the Father is gained by receiving. His love carries everything with it.

However, as a father of two young children, I know very well that they are more than just receivers. As they grow by continual receiving, that vitality within them wants to express itself in growth. They experiment and explore, pushing the boundaries of their existence into more and more life. They have very little self-protection instincts, but they do not need to worry about that. Their mum and I are vigilant for their safety and wellbeing.

In our Christian lives, because we have had an orphan mentality, we had trouble believing that our heavenly Father, the perfect and original Parent, is watching over our safety. In orphan-ness we constantly monitored our own growth, watching to make sure we did everything right and avoided the wrong. The underlying motivation for this was actually fear, and comes from eating of the Tree of the Knowledge of Good and Evil. When we move beyond the dualism of judging good and evil, we can live from our hearts and begin to flow with life.

WHAT IS OUR HEART SAYING?

Another major question that comes up all the time is; How do I live from my heart? When I began to take baby steps in my sonship, I realised that I didn't even know what my heart was saying. Many of us are repelled by the speech of our heart, because it often appears to be negative. When we access our hearts they are often in a state of fear, mistrust, anger and other negative emotions. These may be frightening, unpalatable and painful to face, but it is still our heart speaking. As we learn to open our hearts to the Father, we realise that His love pours into the precise place where the pain is.

In this book I want to set out a way to begin to take steps in living from our hearts. A way to help us walk in the newness of life that is already in us. The life is within us but it is in a seed form and needs to grow. It needs to be lived out so that it keeps flourishing.

When the children of Israel were liberated from Egypt into the wilderness there was very little security. They followed the leadership of Moses and were led by a pillar of cloud, which turned to fire at night. Many of them wanted to turn back to the familiarity of the old because they thought the bondage was more comfortable, even though it actually wasn't. This is where we can often find ourselves. We breathe the delightful new air of freedom, but then we find ourselves at a loss about how to keep walking in freedom. We find ourselves in a place where we have to live our own lives in the love of the Father, in our daily routine. Oftentimes there doesn't seem to be a lot happening. A lot of people are disappointed with the apparent lack of structure and programmed activities, but that's the whole point. We find ourselves in a place where we have to live normal life.

This is the freedom the Father is bringing us into. Christianity is actually about Heaven and Earth joining together. It's about the life of Father, the life of Jesus, the life of the Spirit being manifested in our human condition. God has come to indwell our humanness. I think we've missed out on this a lot, that the whole point of Incarnation, of Jesus coming to live in a human body is actually because that is all God ever wanted to do. God is a spirit and God wants to indwell humanity.

Religion (and, to a large extent, Greek philosophy, which has infiltrated the Church for many centuries) has deceived us that our humanness, our ordinariness, our human weakness, is of no importance at all. But the only desire that God really has is to connect with humans. The whole point of the Incarnation was that Jesus felt the same things that we felt. He didn't come to take us away from our humanness, He came to bring God into our humanity.

For forty-something years I believed that Jesus had come to rescue me from myself, but He didn't. He came to indwell me, and to be at home within me. He came to live within me, ordinary Stephen Hill or, as Randy Clark says, "little old me." That is the glory of God, and that is what we're missing. We cannot see that He is pleased to indwell little old me. But that is the power of Christianity. Many of us cannot live in or receive the inheritance God has for us because we have no confidence in the reality of God within us.

It is quite popular to talk these days about finding your destiny. Much of this plays to our wounded ego and our need for significance. Our God-ordained destiny is to be like Jesus. However, many people are deeply unhappy in normal life because they are not being true to their own hearts, and to that extent, they probably do need to find, not so much their destiny, but deep fulfilment in being who they are truly meant to be.

Many are deeply unhappy and frustrated because they cannot attain to what is calling in their hearts from deep to deep. The mistake that we can often make as Christians is that we can expect the future to somehow drop out of the blue onto our lap. What we miss, and what we have not been told is that the blueprint of our destiny is in our humanity. That needs repeated - the blueprint of your future 'destiny' is in your own humanity. Now I will explore this.

THE INCARNATIONAL SHAPE

I heard someone make a statement recently that got under my skin. It impacted me and I could not forget it, and then I got revelation about it. Here it is: You need to create a shape for life to flow. You see, God needs a vessel, a receptacle to work through. Because God is Spirit, and He lives in the heavenly dimension, He always wants or needs a shape on earth, to be expressed. God cannot express Himself on earth unless He does so incarnationally.

Because God is a spirit, He needs a material shape to work through on this earth. In the Old Testament that shape was a people, a tent, a temple, a Torah, a prophet, a king. The shape that God came through in the Old Covenant was varied in its form, but that shape didn't really express who

God really was. Do you know who God really is in the core of His being? In the core of His being He is Father, so the shape that He needed to express who He really is, is a Son. Hebrews 1:1 & 2 bears this out:

> *"Long ago many times and in many ways,*
> *God spoke to our fathers by the prophets,*
> *but in these last days He has spoken to us in*
> *the person of His Son."*

Now, I made an amazing discovery that in the original language the words "in the person of" are not there. What the writer of the Hebrews actually says is:

> *"He has spoken to us in Son."*

In Son. That is clearly talking about Jesus, but it is not restricted to a particular Person in Roman-occupied Judea in the First Century. 'In son' is about Jesus, but it goes beyond the individual person of Jesus. The language the Father is using to communicate with now is the language of Sonship. That began with Jesus here on earth and it continues with the resurrected Jesus in heaven. But it also continues with all of us; sons and daughters who have an Abba-crying Spirit within them. The shape that the Father wants to inhabit is you, me, all of us. It's the shape of Sonship. What this means is that the more you can become yourself in the love of the Father, that is the shape that He inhabits. His divine life begins to flow through that.

I'd like to share a few things that have helped me become, in some small way, a shape through which life flows; things that have freed to become 'little old me.' Who I am now is actually the real 'me' and I'm becoming more and more the real me. Not everyone warms to or even likes the real me, but that's OK. The more I live in the Father's love, the less I feel the need for human approval. The Father loves to inhabit 'little old me.'

'THE INCARNATIONAL SHAPE'

- Jane

Jane had a life-changing experience when she encountered the love of the Father in New Zealand 2008:

"People want a lot more than 'Sunday-morning Christianity.' They see through the pretence of just turning up on a Sunday and 'doing church' for a few hours. People want something deeper, a normality of connecting with God on a daily basis and getting what you need from Him every day rather than a weekly fix. That model is not sustaining people day by day.

My experience was that I could get my heart comforted and then I could live free, but what the heck was I going to do with a free heart? This is what most excites me.

The mystery of what emerges is going to be unique for everybody. The cry of our hearts has been for the deeply authentic expression of sonship and what that looks like in a very ordinary way. It emerges from that place of heart-realisation and giving room to the heart."

She returned to the UK, and re-entered normal life. Learning to live increasingly from her heart, she began to discover her incarnational shape. Jane wanted to have fun and be more creative. Sewing and design had always inspired her, and past trips to poverty-stricken

Mozambique had really impacted her. She had an idea and was curious to see if it would work. Her idea was to make shoes for the homeless kids in Mozambique. Continuing to work part-time in her previous job, she began to develop a business, Oppi Design (www.oppi-design.com) specialising in handmade babywear.

"I started Oppi in 2012 because I wanted to see if I could do what I love - sewing - and also help some of the children like those I'd met on my travels. Often theirs is a story of survival, but my dream is that they not only survive, but thrive. That they too would have the chance to do whatever it is they love to do."

"Starting a new venture took courage, willingness and humility to ask for help. But what excites me is how, through working together, Oppi has inspired others to explore some of their own ideas too. Opportunity to share expertise and skills is a big part of why I continue. It can be lots of fun being part of each other's creative adventure!"

Religion is trying to get us to stretch up or escape from ourselves to somehow reach God, but true Christianity is the opposite. The truth of the Gospel is that Father wants to come down and indwell us in our strengths and weaknesses, in our gifts and in our failures, so that His life will flow out through all of us.

There are a number of things that have helped me to see the life of God flowing out of me. All His sons and daughters have eternal life, resurrection life, the life of the Trinity within us, but we have been deceived that it is not within us. We have been deceived that we have to try and get it by praying more or by serving more; by intensifying our religious activity. We find it very difficult to grasp that eternal life is pulsating within our ordinariness.

When we begin to be a receiver of the life of God in our weakness, we discover that life of God is resident within us. The thing is, it has to come out and be expressed. When you begin to express His life, you realise that it hasn't originated in you. You find a motivation within you that does not come from your own natural likes and dislikes. You are motivated to love what has been unlovely, to be patient with what frustrated you, to hope in the midst of despair. This change can only be produced by a life that is from another Source.

FREEDOM FROM CONDEMNATION

One of the big things that holds us back from allowing life to flow through us is the issue of being condemned. The major difference between religion and sonship is the issue of condemnation. Condemnation is the power of the knowledge of good and evil. When you get a revelation of your sonship, regardless of whether you feel anything emotionally, one of the major signifiers of this is that condemnation begins to drop away. Paul experienced this when he exclaimed, (in Romans 8:1) "There is now no condemnation to those who are in Christ Jesus!"

We can see from an example in the Old Testament prophecy of Zechariah that condemnation is one of Satan's main tactics to undermine our realisation of our identity before the Father. The prophet Zechariah had a vision which he described like this:

"Then he showed me Joshua the high priest

standing before the Angel of the Lord and Satan standing at His right hand to accuse Him. And the Lord said to Satan, 'The Lord rebuke you, O Satan, the Lord who has chosen Jerusalem rebuke you! Is not this a brand plucked from the fire?' Now Joshua was standing before the angel, clothed with filthy garments. And the angel said to those who were standing before him, 'Remove the filthy garments from him." To him he said, "Behold I have taken your iniquity away from you, and I will clothe you with pure vestments.' And I said, "Let them put a clean turban on his head." So they put a clean turban on his head and clothed him with garments. And the angel of the Lord was standing by."

- ZECHARIAH 3: 1-15

This scenario gives us an insight into how condemnation works. Joshua the High Priest was there in the heavenly realm and he was clothed in filthy garments. We do not know why his garments were soiled. Maybe it was something he had done. Whatever it was, it was enough to make him lose his reputation and to be vulnerable to accusation. The Bible uses the metaphor of clean or unclean clothing to signify righteous or unrighteous acts. What I wish to emphasise is that Satan stood there as the accuser. In Scripture there are only two people who are the named as the accuser, Satan and Moses. The law of the knowledge of good and evil will always accuse and condemn because it will show us that we are never up to scratch, that we never quite make the required standard.

It seems somewhat surprising how this plays out. Heaven overrode the problem of the filthy garments, and the accusation of Satan. Heaven saw the true identity of this man, Joshua, and it was not in the filthy garments. What is also remarkable is that the prophet Zechariah participated in the heavenly adornment of Joshua. Zechariah directed that the turban be placed on the high priest's head and the angels did what he told them to do! Heaven, represented by the angels and the prophet, dressed this man, Joshua, according to his true identity.

In my life, I can say quite freely that my garments became filthy. I fell into moral sin. I lost my reputation as a mature and respectable Christian. Satan stood to accuse me but Heaven saw who I really was and issued the instruction to remove the filthy garments. I received a revelation of purity from heaven itself.

This scenario sums up the insidious power of condemnation. Satan is trying to show us that we're clothed in filthy garments. The arch-accuser tells you that you're either sinning or you're not doing good enough, or you're not serving well or you've made the wrong decision. But those are all points of condemnation and accusation and life will never flow in the face of condemnation. While you are condemned by the power of the knowledge of good and evil, the law and the accuser, you will never be free to flow in the life that is within you. The problem is that most of us wholeheartedly believe that the accusation and the condemnation comes from God, not Satan. We are caught in the trap of condemnation because we believe that it is God who points out our filthy garments. But God the Father never speaks words of condemnation.

Revelation 2:17 contains a promise to the one who overcomes. The promise includes a white stone with a name engraved on it. The white stone speaks of permission granted. In the time when John wrote, one of the uses of a white stone was that it was an admission 'ticket' to gain entrance to particular places and events. The one who overcomes is given access and permission. On the white stone is engraved a name, a "new name... that no one knows except the one who receives it."

There is a secret name that is given to us and it is the identity that the Father sees us with for all eternity. I am not talking about a literal name or some sort of prophetic moniker here. These can be purchased relatively easily. I am talking here about a deep, inner heart-revelation in the core of my being about who the Father sees me to be. About what my unique identity is by His design. Before my garments ever became filthy, before I fell into immorality, I had a 'name' that the Father knew me by. The Father saw that immorality was not the true me.

We are never really free from temptation. It is part of being human in this world. But the true me is someone who wants to be like Jesus. The real me is the one called by the secret name, which is my identity before I was ever a glint in my parent's eyes! It is the same for all of us. So when we begin to get free from accusation we can travel on this road to freedom and for life to begin to flow. Getting free from condemnation is the first step in the walk of life.

LEARNING TO SAY, 'NO!' TO FALSE OBLIGATIONS

The second thing that creates a shape through which life can flow is closely linked to being free of condemnation. It is having the ability to say, "No!" to false obligations. You need to be free from condemnation to be able to say that. Under condemnation we say, "Yes" to doing many things, for example, that our authority figures may ask us to do, because we feel guilty about saying, "No." But our heart needs to say, "No" before it can say, "Yes." Saying, "No" brings definition to the shape that we really are. In the past, I felt really guilty about saying, "No" so I used to say, "Yes" to everything that everybody ever asked me to do, because I thought that's what I had to do! I was trying to do everything that I felt needed to be done, but there was no shape for me to be myself. All of my responses to the need around me sprung from condemnation and I eventually burnt out.

However, as I got free from condemnation, and saw myself in a true light, I knew there were things I just couldn't do, or I didn't really want to do because they were not the real me. The shape of 'Stephen Hill' began to emerge and life began to flow through that shape. Take a cup for example. Look at the cup you are drinking coffee from. It has a particular shape. The chair you are sitting on has hardened edges to it. These give it the shape that it is. In order for life to begin to flow through us our edges need to be defined. It is important to come to this place where you know what you are able to do and what you are not able to do. Lack of clarity in this means that there isn't a defined shape to hold the life in you.

There is a big tendency in our Christianity to have to agree to do absolutely everything, but when you look at the life of Jesus, that there were places He went and places He definitely didn't go. Some things He agreed to do, other places He avoided. He only did what He saw the Father doing. He did not commit Himself unreservedly to every need that arose. In His humanity upon this earth, a shape began to form. The years that He spent in the carpenter's shop were instrumental in forming a shape for His ministry of manifesting the Father. Paul was the same. He became all things to all men in order to win some (1 Corinthians 9:22) but he was able to do this because he had already become free of condemnation and gained the ability to say, 'No' to false religious obligation.

FREEDOM AND THE POWER OF "NO!"

- Frank

Frank was once the international president of a large international organisation, and travelled to over 200 countries as an itinerant speaker.

When I first came into the revelation of Sonship in the Father's love, there was a period of time for "shedding

> the old". This was almost an involuntary falling away of
> things that had once had a basis or foundation within me.
> It became easier to relinquish things that were previously
> held as religious obligations or expectations. Things that I
> felt I was "supposed to, have to, or meant to do" just began to
> diminish and fall away.
>
> As this continued, I was learning how to say, "NO" to so
> many of the little things that I had always felt obliged to do.
> After a lifetime of religious performance I was rediscovering a
> freedom in my heart, and how I could live from there, simply
> by saying, "NO!"

I would encourage you, as condemnation begins to fall
away, don't be afraid to say, "No" when you are approached
to do some things. If your heart says, "No" express what
your heart is feeling. We don't know how to live from our
hearts because we don't know what our hearts are actually
saying. A false 'niceness' prohibits us from declining to
do some things or refusing to go along with some things,
but that false 'niceness' is actually the 'good' side of the
knowledge of good and evil. It may seem good, but it's not
God. That's why I believe we need to learn to say, "No"

before we can say, "Yes." Saying, "No" to things begins to create the shape of who you really are.

In some ways this might be a little hard to swallow, but here are a few examples. In my work life, there came a point where I had to say, "No" to doing certain things because I wanted to become more true to the real person that Father was calling forth. I was able to say, "No" to certain tasks and commitments because I was getting free of condemnation. I didn't want to be pulled into doing a lot of financial administration, for example, because that's not me. What is more, if I agreed to do it out of a false obligation, I would be vulnerable to making mistakes, because number-crunching is not the real me. I knew my own abilities (or lack thereof) better than that, and I knew I was definitely not the person to take up these long-term responsibilities. Saying, "No" gave clarity and defined the shape of who I was, but it also gave clarity to the solution that was needed. Not long after, the perfect person came along to take up the responsibilities that I had declined. At the time, I was still left wondering how I would express myself, but I was beginning to see the formation of a rough shape by knowing what I could and would not do.

Here's another example: When an artist is composing a painting, they make use of negative space. Instead of painting the actual shape of the object they want to paint, such as a vase, they will paint in everything surrounding that object. They paint in the dark 'negative' space so that the shape of the vase emerges out of that shadow. When the rough shape emerges in contrast to the backdrop they can concentrate on the finer details of the object (in this case, a vase) which is the actual subject of the painting. A positive shape is hewn from the negative backdrop.

So the ability to say, "No" to things actually begins to create the rough shape for you to be your true self. David was able to say, "No" to Saul's armour because he knew that it would inhibit the movement of his throwing arm to operate the sling which felled Goliath. By the grace of God, I have emerged with a greater personal life-giving expression, but I had to say, "No" to things that were coming in to steal that away from me. We must come into the freedom of saying, 'No' to false obligations if we are to live authentically from the heart. The ability to say, 'No' breaks the servant-hearted mentality.

WHAT DO I SAY, "YES" TO, THEN?

If we learn how to say, "No" to false obligations, what then do we say, "Yes" to? This is how it worked for me. The Father's love set me free from condemnation into a life were I was able to say, "No" to obligation and manipulation. That took me on a journey towards my heart, but it's not enough to be negative all the time. The language of the heart is a language of "Yes," because the childlike heart wants to discover the fulness of life. Children only say, "No" to things that they don't want to do. Children don't have a problem living from their hearts. The life of a child is one big, unapologetic "Yes!" They say, "No" when they might have to forego the Yes. When my daughter was toilet training I would ask her, "Jessie, do you need to use the toilet?" and she would often say, "No," because she didn't want to be distracted from playing. You see, her default was a resounding "Yes" to life.

How am I going to get in touch with my heart? How am I going to reclaim that childlike heart and live from it? The kingdom of God comes to a childlike heart. I find that God teaches me more and more how to live the Christian life by observing my children. The fact that Jesus placed a child in the midst (Matthew 18:2) is not to be glossed over. Jesus very intentionally used the child as a teaching aide. Maybe we would learn more about how to relate to God by observing some babies and toddlers in our midst, rather than listening to a profound sermon.

PAYING ATTENTION TO TINY DESIRES

How do you know what to say, "Yes" to, then? How do you follow your heart? The answer is a little surprising, and it may be initially disappointing but I am convinced that it works. You begin to find out what is on your heart by paying attention to tiny desires.

If you are anything like me, you may experience a pang of disappointment when I say tiny desires. Our church culture has, I believe, done us a disservice by creating an expectation for great things and big results. Don't get me wrong, I am not incredulous that God wants to give us great things. But I do know that I was hung up in constantly looking for the 'great things' and I was deeply frustrated, even depressed, that I could never get the big vision accomplished, or that I never seemed any nearer the 'destiny' that was often prophesied over me. The fulfilment of the prophetic words was like the mirage in the desert, that disappeared as you approached it. You may not identify with me, but I was overwhelmed by a lot of big dreams 'out there' but I could never pull them down into reality. I could never actually live them.

Where was I going wrong? I was focused on the big stuff, without paying attention to the shape that brings it into reality. In order to experience the greater things, you need a shape that channels life. That shape is created by not ignoring the small things. The road into getting the big desires of your heart answered is to say, "Yes" to the small desires. It's to say, "Yes" to a little desire of the heart.

HONOURING LITTLE DESIRES

- Alice's Story

Even as a little girl, I knew that I wanted to please God, to live a life that brought Him glory. In my thinking, this glory was a vague thing that eluded definition; no matter, the point of my life was to do what He wanted me to do. And so for many years, I pursued His will. Time spent reading the Bible was about discovering what I needed to do for Him, how I could make Him happy. All seemed well in this scenario until anxiety quietly slithered into my life like a great python, gradually increasing its suffocating hold around me. This experience undid so much of what I had understood was the Christian life. All my efforts turned to ash as the fire of anxiety burned up my theology.

In the months that followed, God began to reveal Himself to me as my loving Father and showed me that I actually had a heart. When you are a zealous servant, all you really need is a strong will; however, a beloved child of God needs a heart for Him to pour His love into. What is more, Father began to show me that my heart and its desires mattered to Him. In fact, His life flowing through the unique person He made me to be is what gives Him the most glory.

Far from mere happy thoughts, Father began to show me in concrete ways that this was true. I had always admired those heavy silver bracelets from Tiffany's with the heart on the latch but had never been able to afford it. Around this time I just happened to see one on an online auction. I had never searched for one before but He prompted me to look. I had squirrelled away a little money and this bracelet was only a fraction of the original cost and, with postage, was the sum of my budget. "Could this be you, God? Do you care about the small desires of my heart?"

The closing time approached and, with my heart pounding, I put in a bid. Minutes ticked by and at the last moment, someone else bid! I could make one more bid but no more. As I entered my second and final bid, I said, "Father, if this bracelet is your gift to me, then let the other person stop bidding." Divinely, they did not bid again and a little dream I thought was impossible, came true. When the bracelet arrived in its original box, I took it into town and had the word 'beloved' engraved on the heart for this is who I am to

Him. I have discovered that God is a tender Father who cares deeply about me, and the desires of my heart.

To live from the heart often seems to be too vague, too ethereal to actually live out. In reality, it is the opposite of vague and ethereal. It is found in paying attention to the small things. It is by being honest about wanting that particular pair of shoes, not *that* pair of shoes. It is about trusting Father to provide for the little things first before having faith for the big things. I had to get a revelation that Father was parenting me in the little details of my humanity. I grew in that revelation by honouring the tiny desires of my heart. By admitting to myself that I would rather have *this* shirt than *that* shirt. This sounds very mundane and ordinary, even trivial. The religious or overly intellectual mind despises it. I think it's important, however, because it awakens the heart. It is the little mustard seed of faith from which a great oak tree grows.

So saying, "No" begins to define the shape and saying, "Yes" to tiny desires begins to release the life to flow. As you pay attention to the tiny and seemingly insignificant desires and promptings of your heart, bit by bit you will enter into increasingly stronger promptings of your heart, and you will live more and more from your heart. The wellsprings of life will bubble up and flow again.

For the rest of this book I want to highlight some issues which can be problematic for our spiritual lives and which undermine the outflowing of spiritual life. In my experience these are things which I need to be aware of, and many people find that the life of the heart is hijacked by the same subtle mindsets.

DEVELOPING A SPIRITUALITY OF IMPERFECTION

I have talked about paying attention to tiny desires. They are easily under-rated. Zechariah 4:10 cautions against despising "the day of small things." One of my observations of contemporary Christian culture is that it too often despises the "day of small things." The small things are not merely a springboard to the 'big things.' The small things are, in themselves, of immeasurable value. When we get a revelation of the glory of the small things, we will see God's love manifested in an unprecedented way. You have to believe, that once you're free from condemnation, the desires of your heart are what His desires are. The Father's desire is what your desire is and your desire is Father's desire. Once you are free from condemnation and you come into sonship, you realise that He wants to manifest Himself through your humanity.

The problem with the Christianity that we have assimilated, is that it gives us a message that we need to continually strive to better ourselves. But that is not authentic Christianity. The good news of the Gospel sets us free from the struggle to become better. When we accept that we cannot possibly improve ourselves, we can relax and rest and allow ourselves to be transformed by the only change agent that can make us like Jesus - the Holy Spirit pouring out the love of God within our hearts. Many Christians believe that they are free from religious striving because they go to the movies on a Sunday or drink a few pints of beer, but religion is much more subtle than that. The 'culture of excellence', which is widespread in contemporary church culture, is a subtle form of religion. It is a striving to become better and more pleasing to God.

It was a massive relief for me to discover that God is not particularly interested in excellence. In fact, the opposite is true. God is looking for honesty, for openness, and for people who are at peace with their own imperfections. God is actually quite happy with things that are not well done, because He looks upon the heart. My children are not remotely interested in becoming 'excellent' to impress their mother and me. They love experimenting and exploring, getting messy and creating widespread havoc in their expression of the exuberant life within them. I believe God finds great joy in seeing us do the same. The truth is, none of us are mature as Christians. We are all little babes in Christ. Paradoxically, the more mature you become as a Christian, the more childlike you become.

God actually delights in imperfection. He sees us as little children. St. Therese of Lisieux, who along with Francis of Assisi is the most popular saint among Catholics today, developed what she called 'a spirituality of imperfection.' Her spirituality of imperfection is summed up in her statement, "I am simply resigned to see myself always imperfect and in this I find my joy." Personally speaking, I have found overwhelming joy in accepting my own imperfections and weaknesses. When we accept this, we can be free of having to impress God or pay Him back for what He has done for us. We can then experience His grace, which flows to the lowest place.

THE STONE THAT THE BUILDERS REJECTED

The world system is built on a philosophy of excellence. The religious world system thrives on creating a spirituality of perfection. In Matthew 21:42, Jesus quoted from Psalm 118 to the religious leaders:

> *"Have you never read in the Scriptures: 'The stone that the builders rejected has become the cornerstone; this was the Lord's doing, and it is marvellous in our eyes?'"*

Jesus was, and continues to be, the stone rejected by the builders. What is more, you and I are also rejected by the builders. I am the stone that the builders have rejected because I don't fit people's expectations. I have failed to be a successful Christian. I have failed to be excellent, I have failed to be good, I have failed to do things brilliantly. You see, the world system is trying to build on the stones that are excellent, the stones that are all together, the stones that are self-confident. This is very obvious when you consider the world system in academia or business, for example. We have little problem recognising that aspect of the world system.

But we need to realise that the world system is also the religious world. Jesus in His weakness was rejected by the Romans (the political and cultural world) but He was also rejected by the religious world. He was radically ordinary. He was outwardly weak, but that was the very stone that has become the Cornerstone of the Church. You might think you have not made it, you might think you are ordinary and weak, that you are the stone that the builders rejected but God has you as the cornerstone. God is building something out of who we are.

Personally speaking, I've come into a freedom about this. God is building something out of my failure. He's not trying to change my failure or make it successful. God is using my weakness, my ordinariness, my failure, as a cornerstone. Even my filthy garments, even the fact that I had a moral fall a number of years ago, but here I am. It is part of the cornerstone of my life because the Father's love has come into it.

So whatever is in your heart, whatever doubts you have about yourself, whatever 'accusation' is making itself heard in your mind, the truth is, you are the stone that the builders rejected. God is building His church and building His Kingdom, not only through great preachers and musicians, but through sons and daughters, through people who manifest who He is in every area of human life. All creation is groaning and waiting for the sons of God to appear.

The manifestation of the sons and daughters of God will not be primarily through conferences and seminars. It is going to come through the Body of Christ expressing itself in every area of life, being released by Him into all creation. If you can see yourself as a stone that has been rejected by the builders, you will see simultaneously that God is building you as a living stone. If you can rejoice in your imperfections and surrender the quest for spiritual 'excellence' you will start to become a shape through which life begins to flow.

OVERCOMING THE HURDLE
OF PREJUDICE

Another major issue that hinders the progression of Spirit-life in us is the issue of the prejudices that we hold. Prejudices are the fixed ideas and judgements about what God is like and what He isn't like, what God does and what He doesn't do, or what you or me can do or not do. We all have inbuilt judgements and beliefs that determine our experience of life. I have discovered with a fair amount of regret, that I often missed out on what God wanted to lead me into because it invariably challenged a deeply held prejudice within me.

I find some of the greatest breakthroughs in life are sitting on the other side of an impasse. The river of God's provision and blessing and opportunity is flowing but it is stopped because there is a dam blocking it. That hindrance is usually a prejudice that we hold. This is something God had to deal with in the early Church. In the book of Acts, chapter 10, the Holy Spirit's desire was to fall upon the Gentiles. He had chosen Peter as the catalyst for this cataclysmic event. But there was a major caveat in the way; Peter's prejudice about what was clean or unclean. There was an effective door opening to the Gentiles, and Cornelius was ripe to hear the Good News and be filled with the Spirit, but God had to deal with Peter's prejudice before that door could open. Peter had a vision as he prayed on the roof of the house in Joppa. In that vision he saw a great sheet, containing all sorts of creatures lowered from heaven. Peter was commanded to eat the creatures in the sheet. Peter would have been shocked, scandalised and repulsed by that command. It took the command to be repeated thrice before Peter shifted his prejudice about what was common or unclean.

I was involved in a church many years ago, which was praying fervently for revival, and the transformation of the town in which it was based. Some months later a group of local youth began to come to the Sunday evening meetings. They were typically a bit irreverent and disrupted the service from time to time, but they were hungry to experience something different in their lives. They were actually hungry for God, though they didn't have the language to express it. The problem for the church was that these guys dressed in black clothes and some of them wore upside-down crosses around their necks. The members of the church couldn't handle the appearance of these kids, and actively discouraged them from coming along to any more meetings until they had changed their appearance. What they didn't realise was that God was actually answering their prayer for revival in the town, but pre-judgements got in the way of what would have been something very transformative.

Oftentimes God is opening things up for us which contain massive blessing and fruitfulness, but we consider them to be 'common and unclean.' We have deeply held and long cherished pre-judgements about what God is going to work in and what He is not going to work in.

Peter thought that God would never work among the Gentiles. He needed to have this vision of a great sheet to comprehend that God was actually going to touch stuff that was unclean.

Let me say this; I believe the Father's love is going to take us into places and into things that we thought He was never in. I'm not talking about immoral things, although we may find ourselves in places and situations where we lose our nice, clean, respectable reputation. The love of the Father compelled Jesus to sit among the prostitutes and outcasts of society, to the point where He was accused of being a drunkard and a sinner. My hunch is that our inheritance invariably lies beyond the chasm of our own prejudices. This means we need to get our eyes opened to our own judgements about what He is in and what He is not in. I encourage you to ask the Father to show you where your prejudices lie.

The more that love comes in, the more people can go into places they couldn't previously go into. You see, in the Father's eyes there is no split between the sacred and the secular. You may be hung up on a particular perception of what ministry is and be deeply frustrated because there are no doors opening to you. But it could well be, that your anointed ministry is not within the walls of the church building or the conference facility. It could be that your sweet spot, your deep fulfilment, is with the very people that you have a judgement about. Life will flow when that prejudice is removed.

YOUR UNIQUENESS IN THE FATHER'S AFFECTIONS

You have your own unique place in the Father's affections. You can only experience the individual specificity of the Father's affection for you personally when you open your heart to the reality of your place as a son or daughter in the family. You can only experience His individual and exquisite parenting of you when you are free from condemnation and when the shape of who you really are begins to emerge. Servants do not enjoy the uniqueness of their identity to the Master, but the children enjoy it in the family. Your true Father, who loved you before anyone else loved or failed to love you, appreciates your uniqueness because He created you.

The Father's love for us is very personal and individual. The pulses of love from our original Father resonate specifically to who we really are. He delights in your little idiosyncrasies, and He is fully aware of what He needs to change in you for you to receive what He has in store for you. This needs to be entered into by faith. You cannot know how the Father loves you specifically until you begin to be your specific self. But this will lead you into the body, into interpersonal relationships with others. As love grows within you, love will compel you to give to others.

In servant-hearted Christianity I tried my best to love others and serve others. Ultimately it failed because I had no love within myself. My heart was shrivelled and the flow of life had dried up. You cannot give what you don't already possess. The example comes to mind of when we are in an aeroplane and the safety briefing is given. We are told if the cabin loses pressure and the oxygen masks drop down that if you have a child with you, you need to ensure that you fit your own oxygen mask before you put the oxygen mask on the child. That's the way it works. If

I try to put on the child's first, there is a risk that I will fail because I have no oxygen. I might die but the child will also die. This illustrates what I am talking about.

Many people fall into this trap in servant-hearted ministry. They try to fit the 'oxygen mask' on others before they fit it on themselves, which results in spiritual death for all concerned. In order for love to flow out of me, I have to receive love from the Father first. As a father of children, I am the channel of love to my children. I am their source and my Father is my source. I have to receive the love of the Father in my life so that it flows to my wife and children.

The flow of the Father's love comes in one direction from a single, all-encompassing Source. In my life, I burnt out on too much sacrifice out of false religious obligation, and I had nothing in myself to give. If I don't give attention to the inflow of love in my heart, I have nothing to give to my family and to others. I know when I become irritable and impatient that I need to be in the downstream of the Father's love in my own life. I have to receive the oxygen of His life before I can give it to others.

I think Christianity begins to work that way. If I try and give someone what I don't have it will end up in burnout and death in both of us. This is where you have to be free from condemnation. If you are not free from condemnation you will not give sufficient attention to what you need in order to give to others. When you receive the Father's love for you personally and continue to live in that experience, there will be an automatic outflow to others you come into contact with. Sonship opens up this freedom.

Many Christians are thrown a curveball by what they read in the Bible. We cannot help seeing the Bible as a guidebook to live by. That is a wrong view of Scripture. We need to understand that everything in the New Testament is predicated on one massive underlying assumption. It assumes that the love of God has been and is continually and experientially being poured out. Everything, for example, that the apostle Paul says about serving and servanthood is under the assumption you are already receiving the love of the Father. The same goes for all New Testament exhortations about sacrificial living. Anything in the New Testament that looks like a principle, a rule, or a command is under the assumption of an environment of outpoured love.

I hope this helps you to create a shape, which allows life to flow. My desire is that it gives you clarity and sets you further along that road of freedom. That you will begin to discover the compelling mystery, which was hidden for all the ages but is now revealed. That Christ in you is the hope of glory. That the Incarnation began with the Son of God in the womb of Mary, but the Incarnation continues and expands when the Trinity make their home in us.

Notes

Notes

Notes

Notes

Notes

Printed in Great
Britain
by Amazon